Consumer's Guide to Gold IRA Rollovers and Precious Metals Investing

How to Invest in Gold and Silver to Protect and Preserve Wealth

Bruce B. Downs

CONTENTS

CONTENTS..5

PREFACE...7

RETIREMENT PLANNING 101 11

401k Plans Revisited.............................11
Characteristics of a 401k Plan 12
Individual Retirement Accounts (IRAs) Revisited...15
Traditional IRAs..............................17
Roth IRAs.................................18
Other Types of IRAs 19
Special Focus on Self-Directed IRAs 21
IRA Rollovers 24
Common Rollover Mistakes 25

PRECIOUS METALS INVESTING 29

Gold 29
Gold Stocks and Mutual Funds.......................29
Gold Bullion and Gold Bullion Coins 30
Collectible Coins 30
Demand Factors That Determine the Price for
Gold...... 31
Silver 35
Platinum 38
Precious Metals Investing Tips 40

GOLD IRA ROLLOVERS 43

WHAT IS A GOLD IRA? 43

BENEFITS OF A GOLD IRA 44

GOLD IRA RULES 44

    1. Choose the Right company. *45*

    2. Invest in the Right Type of Gold. *46*

    3. Selecting a Custodian to House Your Gold. *47*

    4. Time Limits and Funding Restrictions. *49*

CONCLUDING REMARKS **51**

RECOMMENDED RESOURCES **55**

GLOSSARY **57**

REFERENCES **59**

ONE LAST THING **61**

ENDNOTES **63**

Preface

Today, our technologically advanced society extols the "virtues of virtual", whether it be the Internet, digital communications, or the fancy gadgets slowly becoming commonplace in our homes.

That being said, savvy Wall Street investors and 'Main Street' middle class folks alike are starting to put aside a greater portion of their hard-earned wealth in hard assets, especially precious metals like gold.

And why not? The gold standard anchored the world's monetary system until the 1970s, and gold continues to be valued for its durability, long-term price stability, rarity, and credibility during severe economic downturns.

After peaking at around **$1,800 USD** per ounce in 2011, gold is hovering around $1,300 as of March 2014. Apart from its traditional role as a hedge against inflation, Americans benefit from gold investing in the following ways:

- Protection against devaluation of the U.S. dollar.

- Protection against a severe banking crisis (e.g. 2008 financial crisis, bankruptcy of Lehman Brothers, etc.)

- Protection against regional and country-specific economic crises (e.g. U.S., China, European Union)

Consumer's Guide to Gold IRA Rollovers and Precious Metals Investing will introduce you to these benefits (and others) of gold investing in the context of retirement planning, savings, and wealth preservation. In particular, Individual Retirement Accounts (IRA) based on precious metal and *Gold IRA Rollovers*.

We adamantly refuse to recommend a 100% commitment to gold, as a diversified portfolio is still the safest way to ensure stable long-term returns. With the volatility of the stock market, and the meagre returns of CDs (Certificates of Deposits), however, Americans deserve to know about these relatively unknown options to help ensure a financially stable retirement.

It's your money, and we want to emphasize professional advice, due diligence and rigorous background checks before committing any amounts to any financial institution or instrument.

For now, do me a favor. Sit down, relax and go through this gold retirement investing primer. In the end, you'll gain valuable knowledge that you and your family will benefit from for years to come.

- Bruce B. Downs

P.S. As an unadvertised bonus, after reading this guide, you can request a **free Gold IRA Rollover Kit** using the link below:

http://edmopublishing.com/regal

Retirement Planning 101

401k Plans Revisited

Way back in 1978, the U.S. Congress decided to do something constructive to get Americans thinking about and saving for their retirement.

As part of the historic *Tax Reform Act*, a tax-deferred savings plan for employees was authorized in section 401, paragraph (k) of the *Internal Revenue Code*. In 1982, people began taking advantage of this so-called **401(k) plan**, and today it is one of the most widely used retirement tools in the United States.[i]

A solid company should have a 401k plan for its employees that offers matching (or near matching) financial contributions, immediate tax relief (i.e. move to lower bracket, deductions), compound savings and earnings growth within your personal tax shelter.

Who could ask for anything more?

401(k) plans are known as ***defined contribution*** plans, because the amount that is contributed is defined either by the employee (a.k.a. the participant) or the employer. Other examples of defined contribution plans include: company profit sharing plans, IRAs, and money purchase plans (MPPs).

Characteristics of a 401k Plan

Some things to note if you currently have a 401k, or plan to start a 401k soon (see **Table 1**):

1. You and your employer must agree on the amount each of you will contribute to your 401k. The 2014 limit is $17,500 for employees just as in the previous year (or 15% of total salary).

2. Your 401k contribution is deducted automatically *before* taxes, which makes it the most efficient and painless forced savings plan available.

3. Companies have various incentives to contribute towards your retirement from the government, plus they may sincerely want to look out for you. Regardless, don't pass up the opportunity for "free" money.

4. A third party administrator makes the investment decisions based on your preferred asset mix, risk profile and the specific securities (i.e. stocks, bonds, money market, etc.) available and allowable by the IRS.

Table 1 – 401k Contribution and Investment Process (Source: How Stuff Works).

Individual Retirement Accounts (IRAs) Revisited

An Individual Retirement Account **(IRA)** has some similarities with the 401k, in that it also a defined contribution plan offering the twin benefits of *compound growth* and *tax savings*.

Americans are often intimidated by financial jargon and use all kinds of excuses to avoid saving for retirement. However, once you understand and agree with the fundamental principles of retirement planning, it solely becomes a matter of discipline to make regular contributions. Then, it becomes a matter of watching your nest egg grow.

There are some basic IRA rules to be aware of, even before consulting with a qualified financial planner:

- Anyone who has taxable income during the year is eligible to contribute to an IRA. However, a non-working spouse may also have an IRA to which the partner may contribute.

- There is a contribution limit for your IRA ($5,500, with a $1,000 catch-up limit for 2014), but the growth in your account is not taxable until the money is withdrawn.

- Money can be withdrawn from an IRA at any time, but the amounts will be taxable according to the appropriate rules. For example, withdrawals from a traditional IRA subject you to your usual income tax rate. If you remove money from an IRA account prior to the age of fifty-nine and a half, you will be subjected to a 10% excise tax on top of the income tax.

- Exceptional life circumstances can permit IRA money withdrawals before you reach 59 ½ years old and exempt you from the 10% penalty. These include: disability, death, education, first time home purchases, medical expenses, and the payment of back taxes. Each of these exceptions still requires that the IRA be taxed at traditional income rates, except in the case of a Roth IRA (**see below**) or an Education IRA.

Traditional IRAs

A traditional IRA should be set up with a reputable financial institution that is authorized to invest your money in various securities (e.g. stocks, bonds, metals, money market instruments and Certificates of Deposits (CDs)).

Apart from the exceptions mentioned in the previous section, you cannot begin to withdraw money from a traditional IRA until age fifty-nine and six (6) months. At age seventy (70) and six months, it must be completely liquidated or rolled over into another instrument. These IRA withdrawals are only taxed as income, so it is considered as income in the withdrawal year(s).

Traditional IRAs may be set up on either a *discretionary* or non-discretionary basis.

17

Roth IRAs

Like a traditional IRA, you can put your Roth IRA funds into many different investments so long as your custodian is prepared to follow your guidelines.

With a Roth IRA, withdrawals may be untaxed. However, contributions to a Roth IRA are not tax deductible, whereas if you meet certain requirements you might be able to deduct contributions to a traditional IRA.

Regardless, there are advantages to owning a Roth IRA:

- There is no mandatory distribution age, i.e. you can take money out of the Roth IRA any time you need it.

- The Roth IRA owner will not be taxed on the money that is withdrawn as long as all the rules and regulations that govern it are followed and respected.

At the same time, Roth IRAs have more restrictive eligibility criteria. Unlike a traditional IRA they are not open to everyone. A single person must make less than $95,000 a year in order to open a Roth IRA, and a married couple must make less than $150,000 to do likewise.

Provide you meet the income requirements, most financial advisors recommend the Roth IRA over the traditional IRA, based on the assumption that your tax bill when you wind up a traditional account will exceed the savings generated by your tax-deferred contributions.

Other Types of IRAs

There are different "flavors" of IRAs, and while you are unlikely to need most of the variations, it's good to be familiar with the main options:

Individual Retirement Annuity – Almost the same as the Individual Retirement Account, but like most annuities, it is set up with life insurance companies instead of banks.

Employer and Employee Association Trust Account (Group IRA): A traditional IRA setup by either an employer, union or an employee association on behalf of its employees or members.

SIMPLE IRA: A traditional IRA set up by small business owners for their employees. This type of IRA is jointly funded, i.e. an employee contributes a certain amount of money and the employer proceeds to match the employee's contribution based on a percentage of the employee's pay.

Spousal IRA – Either a traditional or Roth IRA, that is funded by a married taxpayer on behalf of their spouse who has less than $2,000 in yearly salary. Requires a joint tax statement every year a contribution is made.

Education IRA- This type of IRA is set up to provide funds that allows a beneficiary (e.g. children) to pay for higher education. There is no tax deduction for contributing to this IRA but withdrawals are not taxed.

Rollover IRA – Another type of traditional IRA in which an individual receives a payment from a retirement plan.

Special Focus on Self-Directed IRAs

Instead of a standard IRA, why not consider a self-directed IRA instead?

Self-directed IRAs are fast becoming the American retirement vehicle of choice, because it offers all the benefits of regular IRAs plus asset diversification that better protects you against the vagaries of stock market downturns. It is estimated that over $100 billion USD is currently managed this way, a strong sign that savvy retail investors are already recognizing its value.[ii]

Here are some of the advantages self-directed IRAs:

1. Greater Control: You are in charge of the show! If you feel constrained by other retirement plans like 401k and traditional IRAs, and have the desire to grow your plan like a real business, this is a no-brainer. Instead of feeling locked in by poor management and excessive fees, you decide what items to include and exclude from your portfolio.

2.   Asset Selection: More options to consider like real estate or precious metals, although they must still be approved for inclusion. Note that life insurance policies, personal belongings, antiques and other collectibles cannot be included. Believe it or not, you may be able to tie in a favorite hobby, skill or other life passion into a self-directed IRA and really make it work for you!

3. Better Liquidity: If you need access to your funds quickly, going self-directed means a 1-2 day delay once your request is made versus up to thirty (30) days when having to depend on a custodian who has other clients and priorities.

On the downside of self-directed IRAs are the fees that you will have to pay for a custodian to essentially do less work that a traditional IRA custodian.   For example, some self-directed IRA trusts may charge hundreds, if not thousands of dollars for the following:

- Fee to open your account.

- An annual fee simply for keeping the account open.

- A per asset holding fee.

- Transaction fees for special asset classes like real estate.

Instead of an experienced, "hands-on" custodian making the investment decisions on your behalf, a self-directed IRA account is administered by a specialized, largely "hands-off" custodian involved with a trust, rather than a major investment bank or brokerage. This person's role is merely to keep your paperwork in order and present periodic (e.g. annual, semi-annual) valuations of your account.

Of course, nothing stops you from getting outside advice to make the best investment decisions possible, or even assist you with the account on a regular basis. However, that sort of defeats the purpose of going self-directed, in which case the traditional IRA may be the preferred option.

IRA Rollovers

Rollovers involve a transfer of funds from one retirement account into an IRA, either traditional or Roth. To avoid the twenty percent (20%) withholding penalty on the transfer, the rollover must go directly from the issuing custodian to receiving custodian.

Most rollovers take place after people change jobs and wish to move their 401(k) assets into an IRA. As discussed throughout this book, an IRA will typically offer more investment choices than a 401k in addition to a continuation of tax-free gains and income.

A large number of IRAs only allow one rollover per year on an IRA to IRA transfer. The one-year calendar runs from the time the distribution is made.

IRA rollovers can occur from a retirement account such as a 401(k) into an IRA, or as an IRA to IRA transfer. A rollover can occur into a Roth IRA provided that the individual's adjusted gross income is below a certain level in the tax year in which the rollover occurs.

Common Rollover Mistakes

IRA rollover mistakes can cost you a lot of money in terms of lost growth and penalties for not following the rules. It is still a great technique for Americans to take advantage of, so long as you avoid the following errors:

A. Delaying your IRA Rollover Decision and Execution.

It's important to plan out the steps involved for both taking out money from your current IRA and executing the rollover. You risk a severe penalty if the proceeds are stuck in limbo while attempting to secure a custodian or broker to help you manage your IRA funds In fact, you only have sixty (60) days from the moment you withdrawal your money to complete the rollover. Waivers or extensions to the 60 day rule from the IRS may be possible in extenuating circumstances, but ideally it's best to get the job done within the sixty days.

What exactly are the penalties for a delayed rollover? Missing the 60 day time limit means that the IRS will view your move as an IRA withdrawal, i.e. a regular distribution of funds that will be taxed as income. In addition, if you are under fifty-nine and a half years old, you will be charged an additional 10% tax on the withdrawal.iii

B. Being limited to One IRA-IRA Rollover per year.

Most Americans are limited to one IRA funds rollover per year, so it behooves you and your financial advisor to have a plan in place before getting it done. Therefore, use the necessary time to do your research and find the right custodian. Otherwise, you risk being stuck in an unfavorable situation for the next year, unable to rollover any remaining funds from your original IRA account or the funds that are in the new IRA account.

C. Keeping the same assets in place.

When you execute an IRA-to-IRA rollover, the assets must stay the same to avoid being seen as a distribution. For example, you cannot withdraw funds from an IRA to buy U.S. Treasury bills or gold and then deposit those assets into a new IRA. The IRS would see it as a distribution, because you spent money from the original IRA, and hence would tax your proceeds as income at the end of the year. The IRS would also impose the additional 10% penalty if the money was taken out before you reached fifty-nine and a half years old.

D. Jumping the gun on Rollovers?

Are you risking your hard-earned 401k or IRA gains by rolling over too early in life? Yes, you are.

If you are under fifty-nine years, six months old, you risk the penalties mentioned above (i.e. full IRA taxed as income; 10% penalty). Always consult an independent financial advisor and prospective custodians before putting the wheels in motion. Rules often change on a yearly basis, so stay informed about your rights and responsibilities as an investor.[iv]

Precious Metals Investing

Gold

There are several ways in which Americans can invest in gold, some of which are more appropriate for specific circumstances. Here the main options available to you:

Gold Stocks and Mutual Funds

Consider investing in gold mining stocks and/or gold mutual funds to get a piece of this global, multi-billion dollar industry. Many licensed, established brokerage firms have access to companies from around the world (e.g. Canada, United States, Australia, Russia, South Africa etc.) that offer greater liquidity than gold bullion or coins.

Plus, you won't have to worry about finding space to store your physical gold!

Beware that like all stocks, gold stocks are subject to market vagaries and may in fact behave quite differently from the actual price of gold.

Gold Bullion and Gold Bullion Coins

Bullion refers to "raw" precious metals, i.e. a bulk quantity of gold, platinum or silver as assessed by weight and cast as ingots or bars. Conversely, bullion coins are coins that are found in gold, and kept solely as investments. These coins are not used in regular commerce or transactions.

As opposed to collector coins (**see below**) a bullion coin will get its value from the amount of precious metal it contains and not from the rarity and/or condition of the coin. These coins can be bought from countries and institutions from all around the world, like the United States Mint. The U.S. Mint produces gold and investment coins, and guarantees their grade (quality), weight, content and purity.

Collectible Coins

A seemingly innocent (though popular) hobby could form part of your precious metals investment strategy. *Numismatic coins* (gold, silver, platinum, etc.) achieve their value based on history as opposed to metal content, and for the benefit of serious collectors, must exceed this metallic value to be profitable.

Different people may evaluate collectible coins differently – that's just the way it is. However, there are reputable and experienced dealers out there and it will pay (literally!) to get several quotes before buying and selling.

It's probably better to be a coin collector for fun and to learn about history first. However, as you gain better knowledge and industry contacts, you will eventually be in position to make gains from numismatic coins.

Demand Factors That Determine the Price for Gold

Gold is one of the most highly traded commodities in the world, behind crude oil, coffee and natural gas. Yet, regular folks like us haven't a clue about the factors that determine its price. Here is a list of parameters that you as a "retirement" investor should take note of when trying to gauge this precious metal's value:

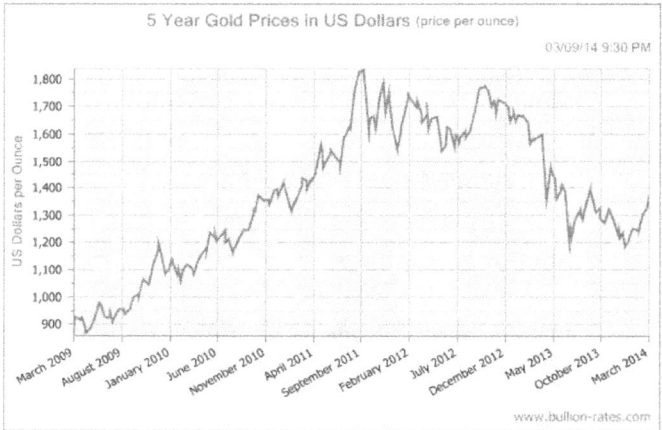

Table 2
Five-Year Gold Prices (USD per ounce).

A. Investment Demand.

Individual investors, institutional investors (e.g. banks, venture capitalists, pension funds) and governments all influence the demand for gold. After 2008, many central banks around the world began increasing their gold reserves in order to back their currency without relying on the U.S. dollar. In recent years, the BRIC nations (Brazil, Russia, India, and China) in particular have made major gold purchases which contributed to gold's spot price almost doubling between 2009 and 2012 (see Table 2 above). Such supply-demand imbalances clearly favor high gold prices.

B. Industrial Demand.

People often forget about the industrial uses of gold (e.g. food manufacturing, electronics, chemicals, etc.). A strong global economy, or at least one in which several major nations are booming can be a boon for gold prices. Advanced technologies also contribute to increasing gold's demand in industry.

C. Golden Jewelry.

Throughout history, up to and including the present day, the majority of worldwide demand for gold stems from jewelry purchases. Led by the U.S., China, and India, jewelry consumption as cultural fashion statements seem to know no boundaries. Pure (24 karat) gold is very soft, so most jewelry is a gold alloy of some sort – including the Olympic gold medals (actually **680** grams of silver with a **960** hallmark and **6** grams of gold with a **999** hallmark) distributed to the winning athletes at the 2014 Sochi Olympics.[v]

D. The United States greenback.

In 1976, the U.S. dollar was effectively taken off the gold standard and has since been the world's fiat currency of reference. Since then, the price of gold has often been inversely related to the strength of the dollar. The 1981-82 recession and the 2007-08 financial meltdown are the prime examples; both of these crises were followed by a steady rise in the price of gold.

Consumer and investor confidence in the economy as a whole dictate how the price of gold will fluctuate (appreciate).

E. Gold mining production.

The current and projected rates of gold production can also influence gold prices.

Lately, world production has declined, and given that most of the world's easy accessible gold had been already been mined, future exploration and exploitation – whether it be in Australia, South Africa, Russia, China, the U.S. or elsewhere – will be extremely capital intensive. Hence, the break-even price for gold companies will likely rise, as will the trading price in the world's trading centers.

As mining technology advances and processing/refining become safer and easier, and as more large-scale projects come online, gold prices may level off in the short-term.

Silver

Silver does not generate the buzz that gold does, but it has been used to generate positive returns for savvy investors. The legendary **Warren Buffett** is famous for making big bets on silver, most notably in 1997-98.

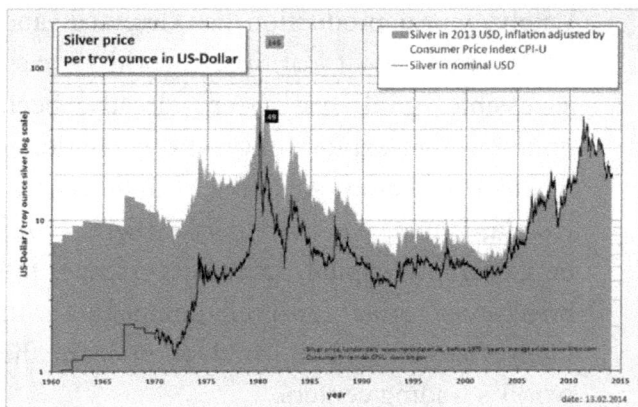

Table 3 – Silver Prices per ounce in US Dollars (log scale).

(Source: http://en.wikipedia.org/wiki/File:Silver_pric e_in_USD.png)

Over the past twenty (20) years, silver prices have been relatively flat, except for two notably spikes (1981-82 (recession; high inflation) and 2010-11 (fallout from real estate bubble and worldwide financial meltdown). The most recent peak price was **$49.45 USD** per ounce in Spring 2011, but current prices are hovering around $21 USD per ounce:

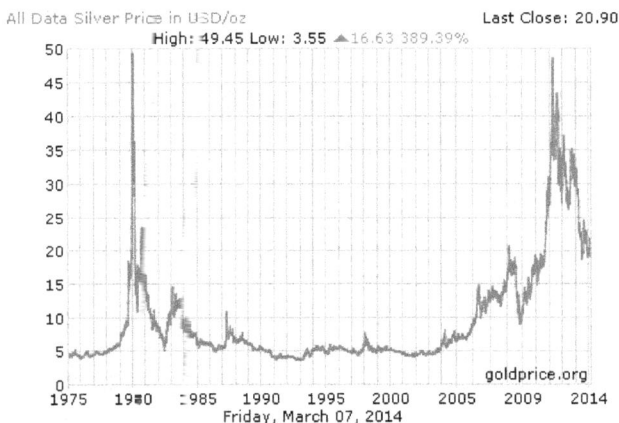

All Data Silver Price in USD/oz   Last Close: 20.90
High: 49.45 Low: 3.55 ▲16.63 389.39%
goldprice.org
Friday, March 07, 2014

Table 4 – Historic Silver Prices, 1975-2014.

Many of the reasons for gold investing are valid for silver, and its value is based on real criteria like legitimate supply and demand (rarity, scarcity) and its near global acceptance as "real" money.

Perfect market timing (November 2008 to March 2011) would have meant a 450% profit over thirty (30) months. More realistically, a monthly investment of $100 worth of silver from 2000 through 2012 ($15,600) would have grown to more than $58,000 for an average annual return of 19% over the entire period (less fees).

37

You have the option of purchasing silver bullion products (bars, rounds, legal tender coins) or rare (numismatic) silver coins that possess value apart from their intrinsic silver value.

Platinum

Platinum may be best known as the metal used in automotive catalytic converters. It does not have the investment history of either gold or silver, but with stocks and real estate still subject to considerable turbulence, investors are beginning to considering this somewhat obscure metal for part of their portfolios. Gold's twenty-eight percent drop in price in 2013 is also a reason for renewed interest.

In fact, the United States Mint issued a press release on March 6, 2014 confirming that it would resume selling its American Eagle platinum bullion coins on March 10, ending a four-year exit from the market:

"The weight, content and purity of American Eagle gold, silver and platinum coins are

guaranteed by the U.S. government. These coins are approved investment products in Individual Retirement Accounts (IRAs) in the United States. [vi]

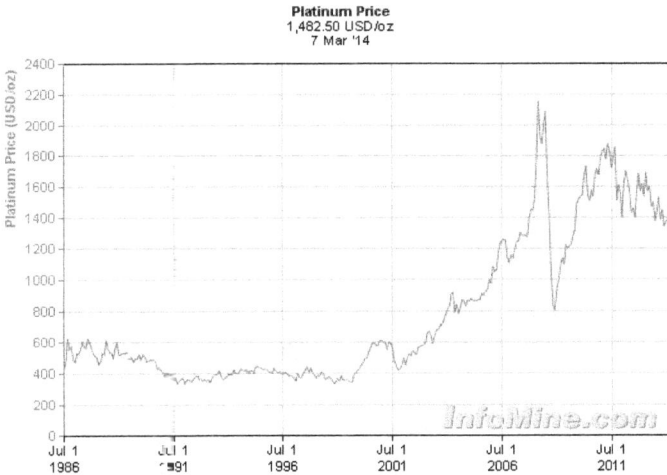

Platinum Price
1,482.50 USD/oz
7 Mar '14

Table 5

Historic Platinum Prices in USD per ounce.

The spot price of platinum approached $2,300 USD per ounce in March 2008, and currently sits just below $1,500.

Precious Metals Investing Tips

When you purchase precious metals like gold from a brokerage firm, keep in mind that they will charge more than the actual spot value. They are out to make a profit, after all! Therefore, compare prices and do enough research on metal values and weights to guarantee that you are getting a fair price.

Precious metals deserve a place in your retirement savings portfolio, but should never be the only asset class you invest in! Gold prices in particular move up and down and can be quite volatile. Therefore, limit your exposure and maintain a diverse group of securities to lessen any shocks down the road.

If you own a gold IRA (**discussed in the next section**), you are not taking possession of physical gold, but instead authorizing its delivery to an agreed upon depository for safe keeping. Nevertheless, you need to make sure that the delivery has taken place as per your agreement and that it resides on site in your name only.

In conjunction with your financial adviser, access the best research and reviews of companies you are considering for investment. Past performance does not guarantee future returns, but a strong track record and proven management are good indicators of consistent money-makers.

It's always buyer beware, especially when it comes to precious metals investments. Learn to take a step back when the sales adrenaline kicks in. Don't rush into an IRA or IRA rollovers, and don't give into pressure to release money unless you are completely satisfied with all the details of the pending transaction.

Gold IRA Rollovers

What is a Gold IRA?

In recent years, the price of gold has risen dramatically in response to turbulent economic times throughout the world. The ever increasing U.S. federal debt, fiscal and monetary chaos in the European Union, and an impending economic slowdown in China have forced citizens throughout the world to reconsider hard assets to help secure their financial futures.

In the United States, the tepid recovery from the 2007-08 financial meltdown continues to way down the real estate market, in spite of near rock bottom prices in several major markets. Antiques and collectibles are another option for folks, but for those of us with '9 to 5' jobs, it's difficult to become an expert fast enough to make serious money.

That's leaves us with the old reliable – *gold*. However, instead of possessing and storing the physical product, *Gold IRAs* may offer you a better chance of growing your retirement nest egg.

Both traditional and Roth IRAs allow you to invest in gold.

Benefits of a Gold IRA

The major benefits of a gold IRA include:

- A hedge against both short-term and long-term inflation.

- **Portfolio diversification** with *real assets*, as opposed to fiat currencies (U.S. dollar) and financial assets that are subject to the whims of a very unpredictable stock market and government economic, fiscal, and monetary policies.

Gold IRA Rules

Purchasing gold with IRA funds does require adherence to strict rules, but together with proper financial guidance, you can gain the benefits of this initiative within days.

Here are some steps to follow when pursuing this course of action:

1. Choose the Right company.

A run of the mill company that offers gold IRAs is not going to look out for your interests. At best, it will purchase the amount of gold you request, store it somewhere (presumably a safe place), and happily slice off a hefty fee to congratulate itself.

Basically, for doing nothing...

On the other hand, a serious and conscientious gold IRA company will take your specific goals and financial situation into account, explain and help you follow all the rules, and ensure that you investment is profitable and secure.

You've worked hard all your life to secure a stable retirement, so check out some reputable Gold IRA companies (2 or 3 minimum), ask the tough questions, ask for references, and choose wisely. (see the resources section of this book for our recommendations).

2. Invest in the Right Type of Gold.

Gold comes in various grades (purity levels) and the Internal Revenue Service (IRS) has issued requirements for the type of gold that an IRA can hold.

"Investment grade" gold must meet these high standards to protect the public from unscrupulous dealers and fraudsters who wreak havoc on tens of thousands of Americans each year through false advertising, fraudulent documentation, and outright theft.

The IRA does allow you to hold gold bullion and bars within an IRA, but insists that it be sourced from accredited manufacturers like LME, Nymex, LBMA and ISE-9000 and be 99.5% pure. Gold coins from a few select countries are allowed, provided they meet the same stringent guidelines. Collectible coins and gold coins not originating from an approved mint like the U.S. Mint are not allowed in an IRA.

Keep good records of the type of gold you are buying and where it came from, because that will determine its treatment for taxation purposes. You must avoid the IRS viewing it as a withdrawal rather than an IRA transfer or rollover. If this happens, you will be subject to income tax on the money. In addition, if you are under 59.5 years old you will be penalized an additional ten percent.

3. Selecting a Custodian to House Your Gold.

A *custodian* is typically a financial institution that holds securities for safekeeping in order to minimize the risk of theft or loss to its customers. A custodian may hold securities and other assets in either electronic or physical form (e.g. precious metals). Being responsible for billions of dollars in assets and securities generally implies that custodians tend to be large and reputable firms.

Most custodians offer a range of services including: account administration, transaction settlements, tax support and foreign exchange. Their fees vary, depending on the services desired by the client. Many firms charge custody fees payable quarterly that are based on the aggregate value of the holdings.

Gold investing requires that you find a custodian who is able to meet the following prerequisites:

- Knowledgeable and trustworthy

- Connected to well-known depositories that ensure space and security for your investments.

- Willing and qualified to handle gold IRA rollovers if your current custodian does not work with gold.

This is why many financial planners will advise clients to go the self-directed route with IRAs. Self-directed IRAs give you the freedom to choose your investments and the flexibility to own precious metals, like gold.

4. Time Limits and Funding Restrictions.

Gold IRA rollovers have certain restrictions that must be observed to be considered valid:

- **Investors must complete the rollover within 60 days**: Otherwise, the IRS will interpret your move as a funds withdrawal and tax you accordingly. Also, you will lose access to both IRA accounts (i.e. the one you transferred money from and the one you transferred money into) for one full year.

- **Limited Annual Funding**: Investors starting a gold IRA are subject to funding restrictions. For example, you can only put in a maximum of $5,000 a year into your IRA. So if you are beginning a gold IRA you must build up the contributions gradually each year. The only way that you are allowed to put over five-thousand dollars into a gold IRA in a single year is through a *transfer* or a *rollover*.

Concluding Remarks

The goal of this e-book is neither to praise nor condemn alternatives to gold investing. In fact, we highly recommend that readers seek out the best investment advice possible and act according to their evolving life circumstances.

That being said, if you are considering a rollover of your retirement savings into a self-directed IRA or to a gold IRA (self-directed or otherwise), start your research by finding company that specializes in IRA to gold IRA rollovers. Many companies may be familiar with IRAs, but only a select few are truly experts with IRA to gold IRA rollovers.

Following the Gold IRA Rollover route demands that you select a company that is trustworthy, offers the best price for your gold, and won't pressure you into gold investments that are outside your comfort zone. Read the reviews of several companies. You should be at ease when discussing your concerns with whoever you choose, and confident that prospective custodians are willing to present you with relevant rollover options.

Need a list of criteria to judge companies offering gold purchases and IRA to gold rollovers? Here it is:

- Reputation: Look at ratings from the Better Business Bureau (BBB), the Business Consumer Alliance, Trustlink and others.

- Great customer service.

- Competitive gold prices, and fast delivery times.

- Low, flat annual IRA fees for both storage and administration, as opposed to graded fees.

- *Segregated storage* as opposed to commingled (mixed) storage.

Regardless of how you feel about gold and precious metals in retirement planning now, the information in this document should serve you well. Americans, even those with limited financial knowledge, cannot go wrong by putting aside 5-15% of their assets in gold (and other metals). Especially as employment and general economic prospects worldwide demand that you do everything possible to protect your family's future.

Recommended Resources

Regal Assets

As one of the country's largest and most respected firms specializing in precious metals for the individual investor and retirement accounts, Regal Assets is uniquely qualified to serve investors interested in precious metals.

Regal Assets has a longstanding tradition of responsible and trustworthy business practices demonstrated by an A+ rating with the BBB and a 5 out of 5 star customer satisfaction rating with TrustLink. Regal Assets specializes in investment advice as it relates to setting up a long term tax deferred retirement plan (commonly called a Gold IRA) and assisting investors in buying and selling Gold Bullion and Rare Gold.

You can learn more about Regal Assets and request a FREE Gold IRA Rollover Information Package at:

http://edmopublishing.com/regal

The Ultimate Bitcoin Beginner's Guide: How to Make Money Mining, Trading, & Investing in Bitcoins

On the flip side of investing in tried and true, safe and secure precious metals is the new, exciting, and speculative digital currency phenomenon known as "crypto-currency".

I'd be remiss if I didn't mention I've authored a book exploring this interesting and controversial form of currency, along with the current opportunities to profit from it.

The Ultimate Bitcoin Beginner's Guide is available at major retailer's including Amazon.com and the Apple iBookstore.

Glossary

Discretionary Account (Managed Account): An account that gives a broker permission to buy and sell securities without the client's consent. The client must sign a discretionary disclosure with the broker as proof of the client's consent.

IRA Rollover: A transfer of funds from a retirement account into a Traditional IRA or a Roth IRA. This occurs either through a direct transfer or with a check. In the latter scenario, the distributing account's custodian writes the check to the account holder who then deposits it into another IRA account.

Transfer ("Direct rollover'): Also known as a trustee-to-trustee transfer, the case in which you do not take possession of funds, since they are transferred directly from one IRA to another. Another possible way this could occur if you receive a check from the old custodian made out to the new custodian.

According to Forbes contributor Jim Blankenship, this movement of funds should not generate a 1099R at the end of the year, because you have not made an actual distribution – hence, no taxable event has occurred.[vii]

References

http://money.howstuffworks.com/personal-finance/retirement-planning/401k.htm (How 401k Plans work)

http://www.certifiedgoldexchange.com/tutorial/silver-investing.php **(Certified Gold Exchange – Silver Investing)**

http://www.forbes.com/sites/ashleaebeling/2013/11/01/irs-announces-2014-retirement-plan-contribution-limits-for-401ks-and-more/ **(IRS Announces 2014 Retirement Plan Contribution Limits For 401(k)s And More)**

http://www.forbes.com/sites/deborahljacobs/2012/06/06/how-to-invest-your-ira-in-real-estate-gold-and-alternative-assets/ **("How To Invest Your IRA In Real Estate And Alternative Assets."**

http://www.goldfacts.org/en/economic_impact/countries/ **(The world's biggest gold-mining countries)** http://www.ira-to-gold.com/open-selfdirected-ira/ **(Why You Should Open A Self-Directed IRA)**

http://www.ira-to-gold.com/regal-assets-review/ **(Regal Assets review)**

http://www.ira-to-gold.com/difference-traditional-roth-ira/ **(The Difference between Traditional and Roth IRA)**

One Last Thing

If you purchased this book from an online retailer (like Amazon.com or BarnesAndNoble.com), you will have the opportunity to rate, review, and share this book on their website.

I truly hope that received a ton of value from this book and enjoyed reading it as much as I enjoyed writing it. If you did, I'd be extremely grateful if you could take just 30 seconds to leave a good rating, a positive review, and share this book with your friends on social media.

It would mean a lot to me; and help others become more educated and informed about planning their financial future.

Thank you again, and I hope that our paths cross again in the near future.

To your safe and secure retirement!

- Bruce

Endnotes

[i] Lee Ann Obringer, "How 401k Plans Work."
http://money.howstuffworks.com/personal-finance/retirement-planning/401k.htm p.1. Accessed 08 Mar 14.

[ii] "Why You Should Open A Self-Directed IRA.", ed. http://www.ira-to-gold.com/open-selfdirected-ira/ Accessed 09 Mar 14.

[iii] "IRA Rollover Mistakes." http://www.ira-to-gold.com/ira-rollover-mistakes/ Accessed 09 Mar 14.

[iv] Jim Blankenship, "What You Need To Know About Your IRA Rollovers And Transfers."
http://www.forbes.com/sites/advisor/2011/04/26/what-you-need-to-know-about-your-ira-rollovers-and-transfers 26 Apr 11 http://www.forbes.com/ Accessed 09 Mar 14.

[v] "About Medals." http://www.sochi2014.com/en/about-medals

Accessed 10 Mar 14.

[vi] Frank Tang, "US Mint to sell platinum coins again due to renewed interest." http://www.reuters.com/article/2014/03/05/platinum-usmint-coins-idUSL1N0M219Y20140305   05 Mar 14 http://www.reuters.com/ Accessed 09 Mar 14.

[vii] Jim Blankenship, "What You Need To Know About Your IRA Rollovers And Transfers.", http://www.forbes.com/sites/advisor/2011/04/26/what-you-need-to-know-about-your-ira-rollovers-and-transfers/ 26 Apr 2011 http://www.forbes.com/ Accessed 09 Mar 14.